W9-BJE-811

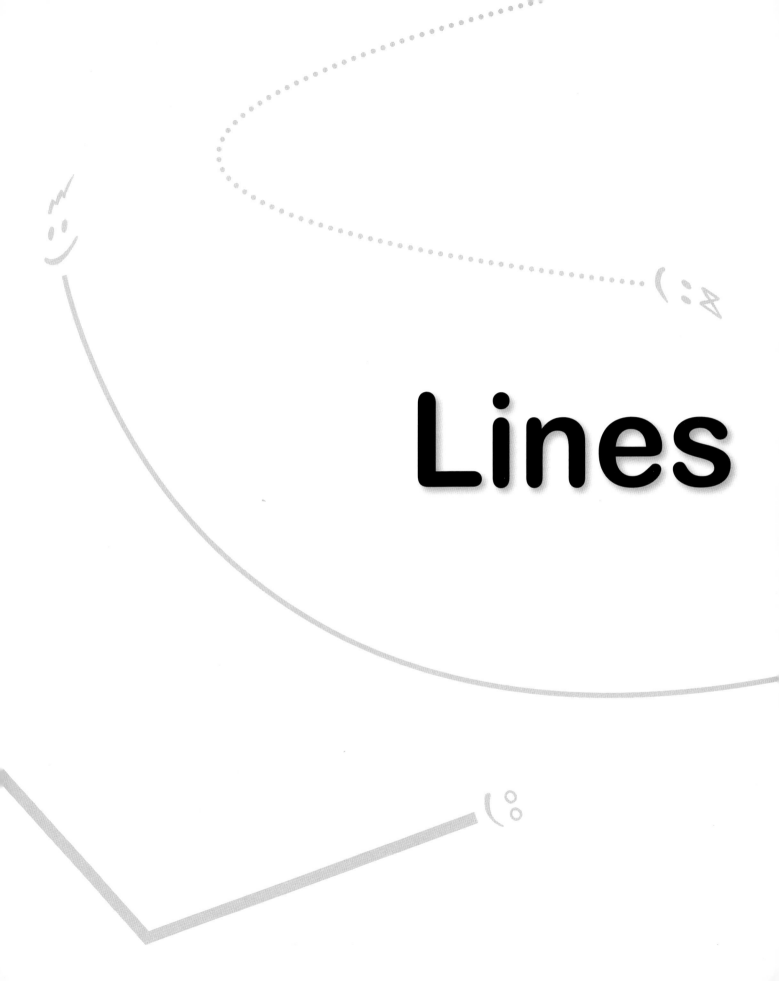

# Lines

**The Scribbles Institute**™ *Young Artist Basics*

Published by The Child's World®
PO Box 326
Chanhassen, MN 55317-0326
800-599-READ
www.childsworld.com

Design and Production: The Creative Spark, San Juan Capistrano, CA
Series Editor: Elizabeth Sirimarco Budd

Photos:
© Corbis: cover
© 2002 Artists Rights Society (ARS), New York/ADAGP, Paris/David
    Heald©The Soloman R. Guggenheim Foundation, New York: 12-13, 30
© Corbis: 16, 17, 19, 23, 26
© Corel Corporation: 25
© Jules Frazier/PhotoDisc: 10
© Anthony Ise/PhotoDisc: 20
© 2002 Estate of Pablo Picasso/Artists Rights Society (ARS), New York/Art
    Resource, NY: 29
© Réunion des Musées Nationaux/Art Resource, NY: 8-9

Library of Congress Cataloging-in-Publication Data
Court, Robert, 1956–
  Lines / by Rob Court.
      p. cm.
Includes index.
Summary: Simple text and cartoon characters introduce some basic types of lines used in artwork and architecture.
  ISBN 1-56766-078-9
  1. Art—Technique—Juvenile literature. 2. Line (Art)—Juvenile literature. [1. Line (Art) 2. Art—Technique.] I. Title.
  N7430 .C694 2002
  701'.8—dc21
                                    2001007642

# Lines

Rob Court

The
Child's
World

Loopi is a line,
a fantastic line.

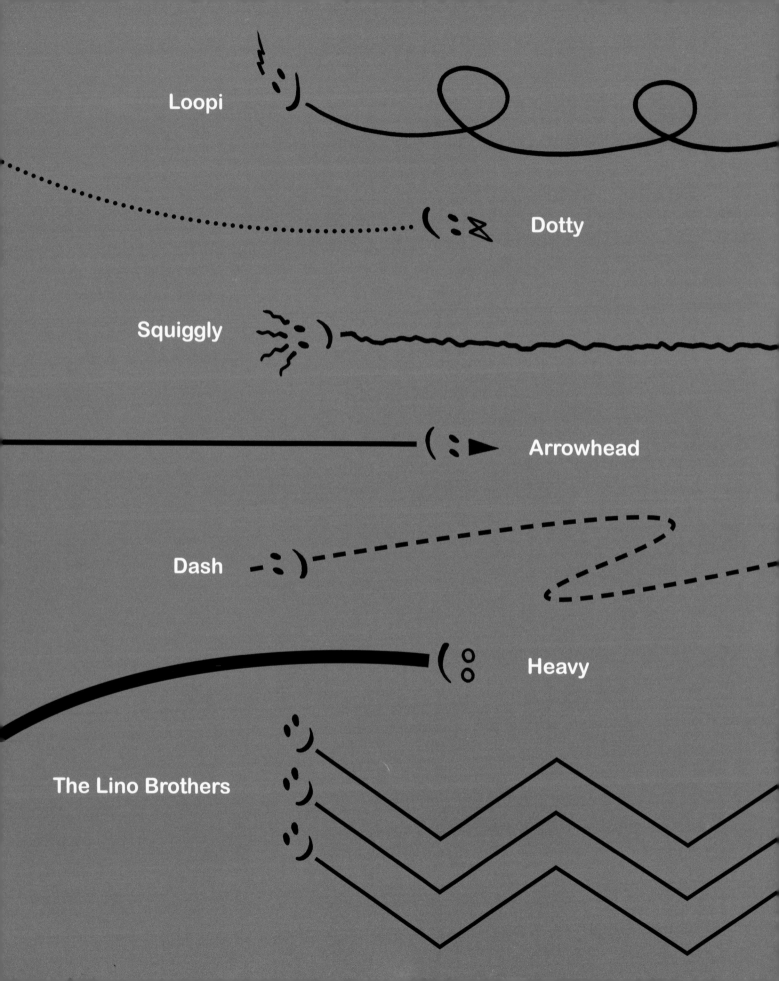

Loopi

Dotty

Squiggly

Arrowhead

Dash

Heavy

The Lino Brothers

There are many kinds of lines.

Some are dotted lines.

Some are squiggly lines.

Some lines point in a direction.

Some lines are drawn with dashes.

Other lines are very, very thick.

Sometimes lines work together
to make **designs.**

Thousands of years ago, people drew lines to **represent** important things. They made drawings with brushes and ink.

We can learn about life in ancient times by looking at drawings made long ago. Artists in Greece created this vase and its drawings almost 3,000 years ago!

Look at the picture. Can you find lines that look like Loopi and Heavy?

For thousands of years, Native Americans have used lines to make art. Artists from the Hopi tribe paint lines on pottery.

An artist from the Hopi tribe made this clay pot. Can you see the different black lines painted by the artist? Can you find lines that look like Loopi and Heavy painted on the pot?

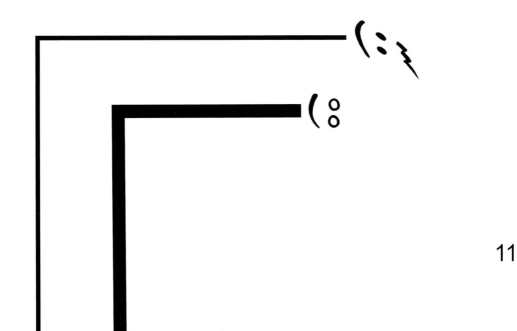

Artists can use lines when they create **abstract art.**

Sometimes art is about movement, color, and design. It doesn't have to represent something from real life. The artist Vasily Kandinsky painted lines that don't look like the real world. He is Loopi's hero!

**Vasily Kandinsky,** *Composition 8,* **1923. Oil on canvas.**

Can you find different kinds of lines in the painting? How are some lines different from others?

13

You can use a flowing line to write your name.

Use a bold line when you want to be sure people will see it.

What happens when you try to write your name while riding in a car?

People use lines every day. We can use lines instead of words to pass on important messages.

What does the line in this sign mean? Where else in the picture do you see lines? What do they tell you?

Can you see a message drawn with lines in the sand?

When learning to draw, artists first learn to see the different kinds of lines in the world.

# Straight Lines

The most basic straight line is called a **horizontal** line. A horizontal line is flat. It goes from left to right—or right to left.

Look at the picture on the next page. Can you see where the sky meets the earth? Where they meet, they form a straight, horizontal line. Artists call this the horizon line.

When you start to make a picture, do you draw a horizontal line to show the ground and the sky?

18

Another kind of straight line is called a **vertical** line. A vertical line goes up and down. Can you see where the darker side of the boat touches the lighter side? It makes a straight, vertical line.

Look closely at the picture. Where do you see lines that look like Squiggly? How are they different from a straight line?

21

# Angled Lines

Sometimes two straight lines meet at a point. Together they form an angled line.

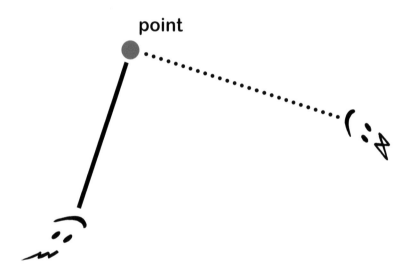

point

Loopi and Dotty join at the point on top of the roof. The lines of the roof form an angle against the sky. How many different angled lines do you see in the picture?

22

Sometimes a line is not horizontal. Sometimes a line is not vertical. When a line leans to one side, it is called a **diagonal** line.

Look closely at the picture of the leaf. Do you see the diagonal lines? Do you see a horizontal line?

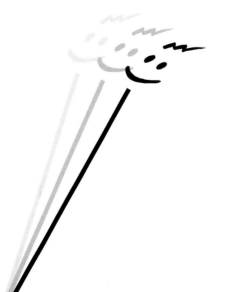

# Curved Lines

When a line begins to bend, it
changes into a curved line. If
both ends of a curved line meet,
they can form a circle.

This photograph shows part of a huge church, the Basilica of St. Peter.
It is in the country of Italy. You can see many designs made with curved
lines. Can you find Loopi and Dotty? What kind of lines do they make?

This line drawing was created by the artist Pablo Picasso. The pencil lines you see are called **outlines.** Picasso used straight lines, angled lines, and curved lines to draw two men.

The Lino Brothers help you to see different lines. Can you find lines like these in Picasso's outline drawing?

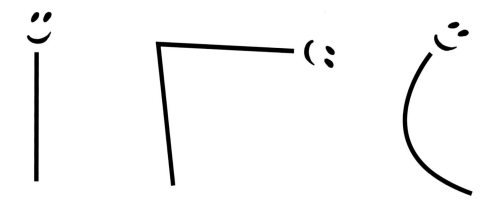

Right: Pablo Picasso, *Sergei Diaghilev and Alfred Seligsberg,* 1919.
Charcoal and pencil on paper.

28

**Joan Miró,** *Prades, the Village,* **1917. Oil on canvas.**

This painting was created by the artist Joan Miró.
He used many bright colors and different kinds of lines.

30

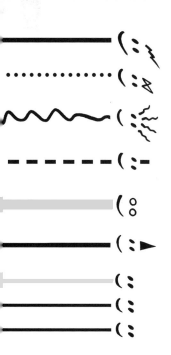

# Put It All Together

Take a minute to study the painting by Miró. How many kinds of lines can you find? How do the straight and angled lines form the buildings? Do you see the lines where the roofs meet the sky? Can you see how Miró painted trees and plants with lines? There are many ideas for you to use in your own painting of a town.

## Make an Abstract Design with Lines

Do you remember the painting by Vasily Kandinsky on pages 12 and 13? What kinds of lines did it use? Try using lines to make a design on a piece of paper. You can put them anywhere on the paper. You can add colors, too.

## Students, Teachers, and Parents

LOOPI the Fantastic Line™ is always waiting to help you learn more about drawing with lines—at www.scribblesinstitute.com. You can get helpful ideas for your drawings at the Scribbles Institute™. It's a great place for students, teachers, and parents to find books, information, and tips about drawing. You can even get advice from a drawing coach!

The Scribbles Institute™

SCRIBBLESINSTITUTE.COM

# Glossary

**abstract art (AB-strakt ART)**
Abstract art uses color, shape, and movement to express ideas and feelings. It does not have to represent objects or people exactly as they look in the real world.

**designs (dih-ZYNZ)**
A design is an arrangement of shapes and colors in a work of art. A design does not have to represent a person or thing.

**diagonal (dy-AG-uh-null)**
A diagonal line is a straight line that slants.

**horizontal (hor-ih-ZON-tull)**
A horizontal line is a straight line that goes from left to right—or right to left. To draw a tabletop, you would use a horizontal line.

**outlines (OWT-lynz)**
Outlines are lines that show the shape of an object. A drawing done in outlines shows only an object's outer lines.

**represent (rep-reh-ZENT)**
To represent something means to show it in a picture. A drawing of a daisy represents the flower.

**vertical (VER-tih-kull)**
A vertical line is a straight line that goes up and down. To draw a tree trunk, you would use a vertical line.

# Index

**About the Author**
Rob Court is a designer and illustrator. He has a studio in San Juan Capistrano, California. He started the Scribbles Institute™ to help people learn about the importance of drawing and creativity.

This book is dedicated to Jesse and Jasmine.